NATURE GIRL

[(X)]

ii

NATURE GIRL

Ana Manwaring

Birdtracks
Letter Press

[(**X**)]

A project of the Broken Nose Collective
Poetry Chapbook Exchange 2019

[(X)]

ISBN paperback: 978-1-7326921-2-1
ISBN ebook: 978-1-7326921-3-8

Certain poems in this book were previously published as follows:

Aspens, Morning Haiku, KRCB Radio 2006
Fire Season, Stolen Light, Redwood Writers 2016
Road Kill, Textures of Love, Healdsburg Literary Guild 2016
Spring, Morning Haiku, KRCB Radio 2006
Dilemma of the Quercus, www.theravensperch.com 2018
Bear Lake, Idaho, Vintage Voices A Toast to Life, Redwood Writers 2007
Clouds, Vintage Voices, Redwood Writers 2006
Turkey Bath, First Press, Napa Valley Writers 2017
The Last Mermaid, www.theravensperch.com 2018
Stone Corral Creek Breeches Banks, Phoenix Out of Silence. . . And Then, Redwood Writers 2018
Rio di San Luca, Venice, Italy, Vintage Voices Four-Part Harmony 2008

Cover design by David K. Prothero
Book design by Ana Manwaring and David K. Prothero

For
David with love
and
Mother Nature—
ever my muse
and
The Broken Nose Collective
[(X)]

Gratitude

Contents

Autumn

Aspens

A carpet of green.
In a deep rocky ravine
bright golden yellow.

Fire Season

The tinderbox of autumn ignites
explosions of oak, of maple
scorches the bark
from madrone from toyon.
Tongues of poison oak shoot up.
With wind flames fan
drop glowing embers
they skitter across
a buckeye softened floor.

Poplars become flame throwers.
Pistache and plum and willow
conflagrate, riot
above fire falls of berries.
Liquidambars,
giant matches flaring,
spark into the vines.
The grapes smolder.

The year, a dowager
dressed for carnival,
summer, her crown jewel
drops
and scatters over the road.

Wood Rats

Autumn rapidly spends its daylight savings
as the leathery leaves of madrone and oak
give way to crackling drifts of brownish ground fog
building up in the hollows of the hills.
Crimson poison oak scatters in the
chill evening wind. Yellow seed heads of anise
death rattle from the ditch.
Swirls of tiny tornados prickle
at my ankles while I trudge upward
        into the big curve.

A dense canopy of dead things
sinewy and swaying and rustling,
illuminate faintly from a tiny moon.
Suddenly shadowed by a dank finger of fog,
a broomstick riding ghoul,
sailing over where I stand
        at the big curve.

Here a galvanized pipe runs under my feet
and belches its echoes into the wooded ravine.
Shivering I catch my rasping breath puffing
from my mouth like a vaporized scream.

The silence is swallowed by the night.
I want to run.

The road is steep and the trees crowd in
their twisted arms reaching down
their crooked brittle fingers
reaching down.

A draft scratches dry oak then silence. I'm rooted
into the asphalt when, scrabbling up
from the bowels of the ditch the rattling weeds,
galloping toward me — my heart pounds —
two monstrous rat-tailed, long snouted hounds of
hell run across my blue Keds,
disappear down the canyon.

The moon emerges
and beams her cool smile.
Heart slowed, I turn up the road toward home
        beyond the big curve.

Road Kill

My heart drags the road,
a net to collect cut-down lives
after the traffic passes.
My heart combs the shoulders,
it rakes the median
and tenderly gathers
the broken bodies:
raccoons, cats, dogs, snakes,
deer, mice, squirrels, birds,
opossums, skunks, frogs —
innocent pedestrians.
How my heart grows weary.

Winter

Eventide

The pale winter sun
drifts to the horizon
slants panes of watery light
across my carpet. I watch
its transit reflected:
gold bleeds into red to flame orange
in my crackling fire.
Outside the light now
fading — amber to butter, spreading
pink to purple to dusk, the embers
of day cooling to ash.

I, by my hearth, flames bright
in the grate, settle winter
into my routine:
the rhythms of hot soup,
long novels
shadows cast.

I turn on the light,
draw close the quilt
and drowse —
dream of the fires of youth.

I had gleaming copper hair.

Winter in the Redwoods

slanted rain
run-off rough
down a ravine
away to the sea
I see
riffles, rapids, eddies
banks cut
uprooted redwoods
giant sailing barges
gouging a canyon
through the misted trees

Storm Surges Under Fog

A tortoise colored sea surges.
Rakes across salted cliffs,
the crescendo as she rises,
her breath foaming—
a chantey grinding stone
to sand in buzzing retreat.
  Fury dampened gray, calmed
  under the tectonic plate of fog.

Impeachment Proceedings

It's a congress in the yard.
A dozen or more strutting statesmen,
sleek in black, heads held high with lofty goals.
The argument voiced, some
turn away, meet in small groups
of much flapping and cawing.
When a fat one tweets *no quid pro quo*
partisans take the floor—
raucous debate, noisy tussle,
head feathers a war bonnet crowning
feints and challenges—
bird-dogging alliances.
Then some know-it-all
runs into the middle of the fracas
to bully a freshman.
It's looking like murder,
until the Speaker
squawks out from a tree,
Lunch recess! Lunch!
And they turn their beaks to the worms.

The Moon Sees
January 2018

Luna weeps for what she sees,
draws a dark veil across
the mirror of her placid face.
Rhythm of time suspended
she arcs the path of totality.
Her reflection dims with
the mist of her tears rising
up from the dying earth.

I tilt high my head to watch her
now amid a lambent corona.

Luna illuminates our shame
as she opens the curtain
wide.

Her blood red cheeks burn,
But her rage flush fades
behind the headlights and noise as
humans, unseeing,
rise to meet the new day.

Spring

Spring

Tiny soft blessings
fluttering down upon us
like spent plum petals

The Dilemma of the Quercus
Or Oak Erotica

You elongate your catkins,
male flowers dangled
from the tips of your naked limbs
in seduction of the wind before Spring
unfurls your pink or chartreuse canopy.
Your few females tuck up at the crook,
nondescript, awaiting the ecstasy of pollen.

Monoecious yet self-incompatible
you must count on your distant-relations
standing near, and the hillsides
abreeze in ochre, or the powdered
buzz of native bees
to deliver the yellow dust
that pollinates life into your acorns
to grow fine new trees.

The Question

What question wafts on the spring air
like feathered seed, trailing the chatter
of grey squirrels from the redwoods, twittering
with the finches in leafy hiding, awaiting
Sunday brunch at the feeder?
A question cooed in ringed doves sacred song.
A question as iridescent and sleek
as that pair of crows, calling
plans for offspring growing
in egg sacs nearby.
Does the family of quail pecking
across the field answer?

Moon Phase

Cool light does not judge;
She sees it all, good and bad.
New moon smiles earthward.

Full moon shines earthward.
Silver light illuminates,
Leaving judgment to humans.

Awakening

It's twenty to eight
on an evening in late April.
The eucalyptus silhouette
against Sonoma Mountain,
load the cumbersome bodies
of turkeys.

Daylight fades; the Blue family chatters.

Since winter, I've seduced a triplet of crows
with food and charms.
They chide me from the trees
yet they come.
I await their shiny crow gifts.
Am I not the provider of corn?

The denizens of my acre roost or wake.

Dusk transits into night;
Too cold to linger. I slide
the door closed, flip on the light
illuminate the pair of skunks
feeding on leavings
of white crested sparrows,
towhees, purple house finches,
banded doves.

Striped backs turn, feathery tails lift.
I toss diced apple.

They sniff-out the delicacy, nod
to the opossum, a baby on her back.

Alison, tail erect, rushes in,
head butts me.
Hungry she herds me
to crown her kibble with Greenies.
Almost as tasty as the gophers
she'll hunt with the owls
on the night-shift.

Spirit

The breeze ruffles the eucalyptus
tousles the box oaks outside my window.
The Cooper's hawk cries for a mate.
I breathe the blossom scented air
warm in the paths of sunlight
that ease across my studio floor
with the afternoon.

Be filled.

Summer

Bear Lake, Idaho

Half dozing across miles of
straw-colored chaparral in the back seat
of an apple-green Ford woody
with the windows wide open.
Snippets of my parents' conversation
blown back,
warm wind chasing their words
into the camping gear
stowed behind me.

We were crowded
sticking to the plastic bench.
My brother wedged between us sisters,
feet resting on the driveshaft hump.
5o miles per hour so fast as we motored
across dusty plateaus,
into dry canyons, red and crumbling.
Up and down the tarmac track
rolling over hills stretching yellow
under a water-colored sky
the rising and falling grass corralled
horizon to horizon.

Soothed by the scent of hay and sage
on the rush of the wind, I fell
into a dream lush and sweet as ripe fruit. I became a
flowing-haired queen upon a sorrel horse
bejeweled in sapphires, diamonds, gold, and
turquoise — the watery jewel in the distance winked,
catching my inward eye.

I would wear such a gem
as that, nestled down this golden slope
and offered up like the promise of heaven.

Waiting

Sun dapples through the willow
trailing over the patio,
the patchy warmth inviting.
Alison stretching out
to soak in the morning,
sleek fur shooting rainbows
as a ray strikes.
Her eyes are closed,
but her whiskers twitch
each time one of the tiny yellow birds
lands on the feeder.
Too much effort to leap
for the bright plumage.
She'll doze and watch
until the deck rotates to shade
and the ground feeders:
the crested sparrows
the tempting towhees
the sweet plump doves,
flock
to the spilled seed
left behind.

Clouds

Clouds sweep smooth across the sky.
The initiate combs the sand
Of Buddha's garden
Separating the smooth clouds
Into wisps of marabou.

Turkey Bath

A scatter of purple finches shelter into the oak
as I thunder down the rickety wooden stairs
to chase the turkeys away.
I breathe in the astringent pure air
of harlequin eucalyptus bowing with
the weight of a murder of chatting crows.
absorb the warmth of the sun,
exhale my irritation.
The flock's bathing habits—
another coneflower raked
from its bowl of soft earth
to make a dust bath.
I hear them now, in the trees,
the turkeys softly whistling a warning.
I stop, turn back to the stair.
Today is God's day,
and anyway
the fox slowly culls the flock.

Warming

The Last Mermaid

Fresno police are seeking
the public's help in identifying a woman
found wet and mostly naked, walking
down a road near a lake
early Tuesday morning.
The woman says her name is Joanna;
she's a mermaid.
Authorities say she answered questions, "I don't
know," but she does have two webbed toes on each
foot.

My pond shrinks,
silted, cracked in the warming.
My sea filled-in,
its shores a distant yearning.

I'm Joanna, the last to survive.

I've watched the tumult of humankind
drown out the siren's song
as it shoals the great ocean.
Now tract homes and shopping malls,
movieplexes and office parks,
golf courses and auto rows, surround
the few salted puddles remaining.

Desiccated, my once lithe fin
chipped to webbed nubs
carries me away from my tiny mere.
Through this desert air I limp. Parched.
Just a drop of clean water to moisten my tongue,
just a drop to help me remember my song.
I don't know.
I don't know

Stone Corral Creek Breaches Banks
Maxwell, CA 2/20/17

No one outside town seems to care
Swift's Stone Corral is flooded and closed,
swamped from history.
The swollen land can't take any more rain
after so long without.

At two a call, "bring the boat,
the creek's spilled over."
Eleven hundred three souls evacuated
ferried to hills beyond the rain-swelled
rice paddies, to watch through graying dawn
the crop swept along the current.
Men waded from the Old Maxwell Saloon,
helped to shutter and sandbag.
These, the almond farmers,
looked on as rain pelted early blossoms
to soggy ground.

Stone Corral Creek Breaches Banks
A tiny farming town washes in muddy run-off:
a river of pesticides and fertilizers and farm debris.
In three hundred-sixty five homes
the folk pack their soggy possessions,
load into the rescue boats and drift
across their fields, washing up
like flotsam onto higher shores.

Venice

Gondola glissade over murky thick glass
through corridors of corroded pastel plaster.
Perfumed green with garbage, seaweed,
and rising tide.

Voices echo.
The banging of shutter, sharp
high up the canyon wall,
and melancholy accordion chords
drift like flotsam in the wake.

Rotten doors and rotted gates,
waterlogged and dressed in slime,
hang mossy and corrupt.

No longer
the elegant foot of a suitor
beneath silk *bauta*, steps
lightly up the stair, nor reveler,
costumed and masked behind paper and gesso,
swirls through gilt halls.
Vivaldi haunts the warm evening air
where no lovers embrace on iron balconies
nor clip of rebuffed heel sounds on cobble.

A solitary pink petal
swirls on a trace of light.
Landing in the current,
it is pulled into the sea.

Golden reflections of yesterday,
Venice drowns
beneath the sun.

Adaptation

You wouldn't know it
but those marauders
picking over your middens
your pantries
your storerooms
your gardens,
they used to be trapped,
incarcerated, exterminated.

It wasn't like now, the vermin
in competition for our tenuous survival:
the dwindling water
exhausted resources
the determined sprouts
poking through grey soil.

No, before this change
you knew the rat was sick when
it appeared on the patio staggering,
its belly filled with too much birdseed.

The Empty Bee Box

The sun a spotlight on my metal chair warming
my face tilted up to soak the afternoon's silence
as sun and land secretly conspire to riotous disorder
sprouting and blooming and bringing forth bees
and ants, gopher snakes and the pair of crows to forage
to mate; my garden their abundant future.

Yet politicians scupper Earth's viable future
creatures too busy living to anticipate global warming
as habitats shrink and humans mismanage the forage
and crops, poisoning for profit the natural world to silence
unconcerned with topics of little interest like bees
and their Honey Bee Colony Collapse Disorder.

Children of Earth—all affected by this disorder.
Without our pollinators we have no future.
With every bite of dinner remember the bees
industrious from blossom to flower that teem in the
warming
spring after the sluicing winter, their tiny buzzing silence
shrinking, a muted reminder of loss of nutritious forage.

Incomprehensible and cruel this throwing off of forage
this dismissal of reality as Earth spirals to disorder.
The presidential request of scientists' silence,
the denial we have nothing but a bright future
making America great as global warming
dries farmlands to dust and starving the bees,

Already confused by neonicotinoids, bees
losing their way, unable to fly from forage
to hive. Monsanto, Dow, Bayer aiding the warming
with aggressive pesticides that cause disorder
to the natural cycle. Only super viruses survive the future
as Varroa, the destructor parasite sends bees to silence.

We must tabulate the evidence and fill the silence
with the real news. Gone the clover, the alfalfa. Our bees
are starving and the almond crop is dwindling. In our
          future:
the memory of honey and butter spread on hot toast as we
          forage
the cupboard for a remnant of natural food, but find
          disorder
of empty plastic containers, the leavings of the Earth's
          warming.

I offer the other beings my acre of forage.
My bees and I are saving seed for the coming disorder.
To plant a field of wildflowers — my policy for warming.

About the author:

Ana teaches creative writing and autobiographical writing through Napa Valley College in California's wine country. She is the founder of JAM Manuscript Consulting where she coaches writers, assists in developing projects and copyedits.

www.ingramcontent.com/pod-product-compliance
Lightning Source LLC
Chambersburg PA
CBHW020443030426
42337CB00014B/1370